my itty-bitty bio

Ida B. Wells

Published in the United States of America by Cherry Lake Publishing
Ann Arbor, Michigan
www.cherrylakepublishing.com

Reading Adviser: Marla Conn, MS, Ed, Literacy Specialist, Read-Ability, Inc.
Book Designer: Jennifer Wahl
Illustrator: Jeff Bane

Photo Credits: © Ingo70/Shutterstock.com, 5; Public Domain/Garrity, Mary [circa 1893], Restored by Cuerden, Adam/Wikimedia, 7; ©Library of Congress/Reproduction No. LC-DIG-ppmsc-00199/Delano, Jack [1940], 9, 22; © Project Gutenberg/Wikimedia, 11; Wells, Ida B. Papers, [Box 10, Folder 1], Special Collections Research Center, University of Chicago Library/Wikimedia, 13; © Athena LeTrelle/Flickr, 15, 23; Wikimedia/Harriet Anderson Stubbs Murphy [1902], 17; © Library of Congress/Reproduction No. LC-USZ62-51555, 19; © neftali/Shutterstock.com, 21; Cover, 1, 8, 10, 18, Jeff Bane; Various frames throughout, ©Shutterstock Images

Library of Congress Cataloging-in-Publication Data

Names: Spiller, Sara, author. | Bane, Jeff, 1957- illustrator.
Title: Ida B. Wells / Sara Spiller ; illustrator, Jeff Bane.
Description: Ann Arbor, Michigan : Cherry Lake Publishing, 2019. | Includes bibliographical references and index.
Identifiers: LCCN 2018034513| ISBN 9781534142725 (hardcover) | ISBN 9781534140486 (pdf) | ISBN 9781534139282 (pbk.) | ISBN 9781534141681 (hosted ebook)
Subjects: LCSH: Wells-Barnett, Ida B., 1862-1931--Juvenile literature. | African American women civil rights workers--Biography--Juvenile literature. | Civil rights workers--United States--Biography--Juvenile literature. | African American women educators--Biography--Juvenile literature. | African American women journalists--Biography--Juvenile literature. | United States--Race relations--Juvenile literature. | African Americans--Civil rights--History--Juvenile literature. | African Americans--Social conditions--To 1964--Juvenile literature. | Lynching--United States--History--Juvenile literature.
Classification: LCC E185.97.W55 S69 2019 | DDC 323.092 [B] --dc23
LC record available at https://lccn.loc.gov/2018034513

Printed in the United States of America
Corporate Graphics

table of contents

About the author: Sara Spiller is a native of the state of Michigan. She enjoys reading comic books and hanging out with her cats.

About the illustrator: Jeff Bane and his two business partners own a studio along the American River in Folsom, California, home of the 1849 Gold Rush. When Jeff's not sketching or illustrating for clients, he's either swimming or kayaking in the river to relax.

my story

I was born in Mississippi.

It was 1862.

WELCOME TO
MISSISSIPPI
Birthplace of America's Music

My parents and one brother died. They had **yellow fever**. I was 16 and the oldest. I took over caring for my five brothers and sisters.

How do you take care of others?

I was a schoolteacher. I was traveling to work. I bought a **first-class** train ticket.

I was told to sit in the area for blacks. I refused to move. I was forced off the train.

Why was this unfair?

I wanted to fight **racism**. So I wrote about it. I wrote many articles. I wrote about **civil rights**. I wrote about giving women the right to vote.

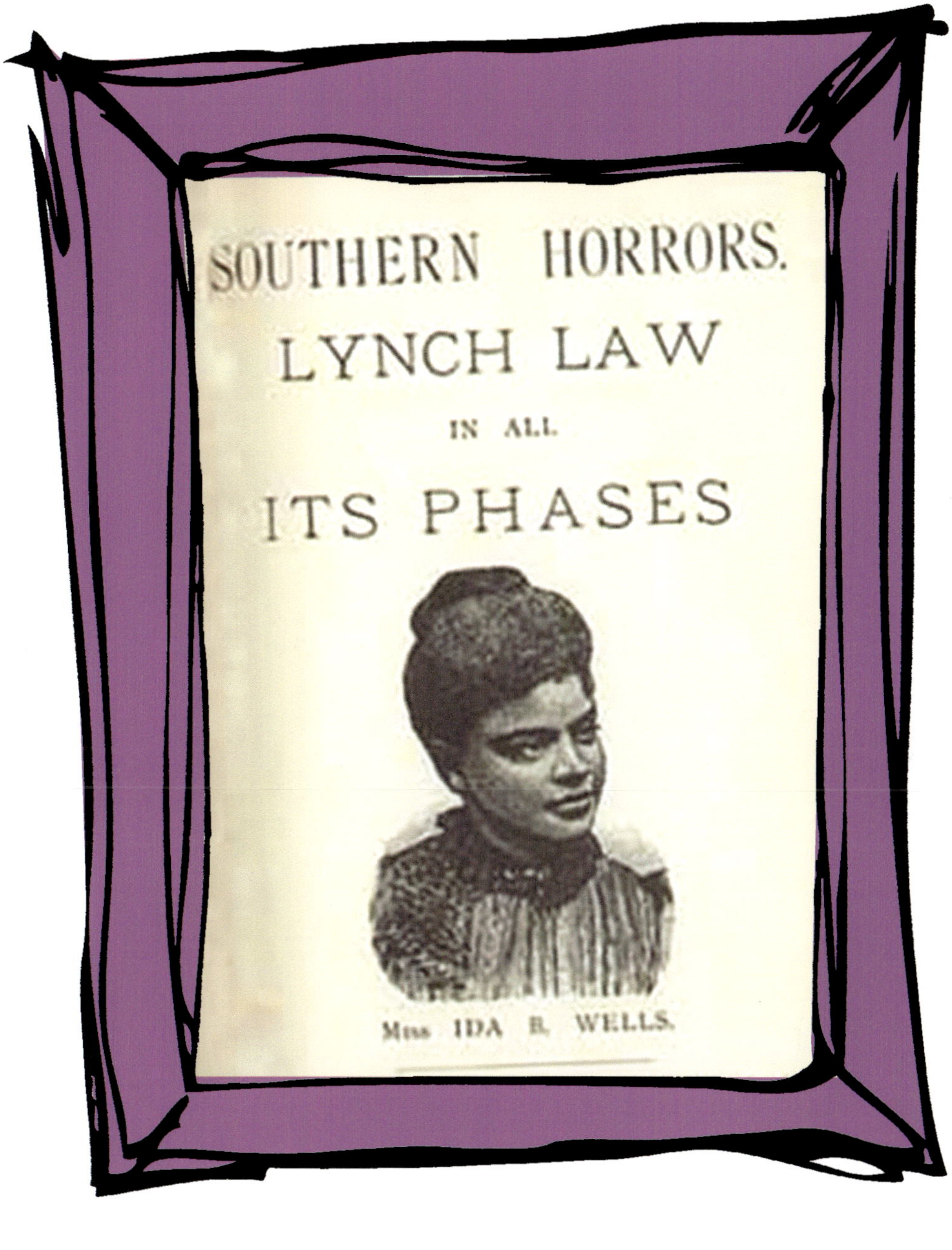

SOUTHERN HORRORS.
LYNCH LAW
IN ALL
ITS PHASES

Miss IDA B. WELLS.

I met Ferdinand Lee Barnett. He started the first black newspaper in Chicago, Illinois. We fell in love. We married and had children.

Three of my black friends were killed. I was upset. Their deaths made me take more action.

A MAN WAS
LYNCHED
YESTERDAY

I sent a message to President William McKinley.

I wanted him to create laws. I wanted him to keep black people safe.

What would you tell
your president?

I helped start a group for black people. I started another group just for black women. I wanted to end unfairness toward black people. I also wanted women to have the right to vote.

I wrote a book before I died.
The book is about my life.
It is about what I fought for.
It is about fighting for fairness.
I died in 1931.

I **inspired** people. I wanted everyone to have the same **rights**.

What would you like to ask me?

timeline

1884

1860

Born
1862

1892

1960

Died
1931

glossary & index

glossary

civil rights (SIV-uhl RITES) the rights all people should have regardless of their differences

first-class (furst-KLAS) the best type of something

inspired (in-SPYRD) filled someone with a strong feeling or an idea

racism (RAY-sih-zum) when people think their race is better than other races and treat those people worse

rights (RITES) the freedom to do something by law

yellow fever (YEL-oh FEE-vur) a sickness spread by mosquitoes

index